INFANTA

Infanta

ERIN BELIEU

COPPER CANYON PRESS

Copyright © 1995 by Erin Belieu.

Publication of this book is supported by a grant from the National Endowment for the Arts and a grant from the Lannan Foundation. Additional support to Copper Canyon Press has been provided by the Andrew W. Mellon Foundation, the Lila Wallace–Reader's Digest Fund, and the Washington State Arts Commission. Copper Canyon Press is in residence with Centrum at Fort Worden State Park.

Library of Congress Cataloging-in-Publication Data
Belieu, Erin, 1965–
Infanta / Erin Belieu.
p.   cm.
ISBN 1-55659-101-2 (pbk.)
I. Title.
PS3552.E479I54 1995
811'.54 – DC20   95-14192

0 9 8 7 6 5 4 3 2

COPPER CANYON PRESS
P.O. BOX 271, PORT TOWNSEND, WASHINGTON 98368

Grateful acknowledgment goes to the magazines in which these poems have appeared:

AGNI: "For Catherine: Juana, Infanta of Navarre"

The Antioch Review: "Rondeau at the Train Stop"

The Formalist: "The Spring Burials:

Greensboro Review: "The Silver Tree"

Harvard Review: "*from* The Exploding Madonna"

The Journal: "The Man Who Tried to Rape You," "A Sleeping Man Must Be Awakened to Be Killed," "All Distance," "Outside the Hotel Ritz," "Bee Sting," "Tick," "The Dream After Surgery," and "The Rescue Ship"

The Laurel Review: "The Green That Never Leaves the Skin"

The Nebraska Review: "The Death of Humphrey Bogart," "You Come Too...," and "The Hideous Chair"

ONTHEBUS: "The Sadness of Infidels"

Salamander: "Georgic on Sitting Still" and "Lullaby For a Russian Painter"

Yellow Silk: The Journal of the Erotic Arts: "Erections," "Prayer For Men," and "The Real Animal"

I would also like to thank (chronologically!) those people whose affection, support and constructive criticism have helped immeasurably in the writing of these poems: Mike Gaherty, Kay Auxier-Horwath, Jim Horwath, Catherine Paciotti, Richard Duggin, Art Homer, Susan Aizenberg, Michelle Herman, Kathy Fagan, Jeredith Merrin, Elizabeth Taylor, Alfred Corn, Edward Hirsch, Carl Phillips, Doug Macomber, Don Share, John Mulligan, Richard Curtis, Askold Melnyczuk and Bruce Smith.

A special thanks to Robert Pinsky, Derek Walcott, Daniel Halpern and Amanda Ford at the NPS, Sam Hamill and the good folks at Copper Canyon and Hayden Carruth who believed in my work and made this book possible.

This book is for Wendell, Margaret, and Dennis Belieu,
and for Joe Osterhaus.

Contents

I

5 Georgic on Memory
7 Legend of the Albino Farm
9 Part of the Effect of the Public Scene
11 All Distance
13 The Spring Burials
14 The Small Sound of Quiet Animals
16 Outside the Hotel Ritz
17 Names You Can't Pronounce
19 Rondeau at the Train Stop
20 The Hideous Chair

II

25 For Catherine: Juana, Infanta of Navarre
27 Another Poem for Mothers
29 Bee Sting
30 *from* The Exploding Madonna
36 Erections
38 Rose Red
40 Ordinary Storm
42 The Green That Never Leaves the Skin
44 Prayer for Men
45 The Problem of Fidelity
46 A Sleeping Man Must Be Awakened to Be Killed
48 Love Poem
49 The Sadness of Infidels
50 The Real Animal
52 You Come Too...
53 Tick

III

57 The Man Who Tried to Rape You
59 The Dream, After Surgery
61 Georgic on Sitting Still
63 Teaching Madeleine to Swim
64 Lullaby for a Russian Painter
65 The Rescue Ship
67 How the Elderly Drive
68 On Being Disregarded by the Famous
70 The Silver Tree
72 The Death of Humphrey Bogart

...But can a woman, pressed by memory's finger,
In the deep night, alone,
Of her softness move
The airy thing
That presses upon her
With the whole weight of love?...

BABETTE DEUTSCH,
FROM "NATURAL LAW"

INFANTA

I

Georgic on Memory

Make your daily monument the Ego,
use a masochist's epistemology
of shame and dog-eared certainty
that others less exacting might forgo.

If memory's an elephant, then feed
the animal. Resist revision: the stand
of feral raspberry, contraband
fruit the crows stole, ferrying seed

for miles... No. It was a broken hedge,
not beautiful, sunlight tacking
its leafy gut in loose sutures. Lacking
imagination, you'll take the pledge

to remember – not the sexy, new
idea of history, each moment
swamped in legend, liable to judgment
and erosion; still, an appealing view,

to draft our lives, a series of vignettes
where endings could be substituted –
your father, unconvoluted
by desire, not grown bonsai in regret,

the bedroom of blue flowers left intact.
The room was nearly dark, the streetlight
a sentinel at the white curtain, its night
face implicated. Do not retract

this. Something did happen. You recall,
can feel a stumbling over wet ground,

the cave the needled branches made around
your body, the creature you couldn't console.

Legend of the Albino Farm

Omaha, Nebraska

They do not sleep nights
but stand between

rows of glowing corn and
cabbages grown on acres past

the edge of the city.
Surrendered flags,

their nightgowns furl and
unfurl around their legs.

Only women could be this
white. Like mules,

they are sterile
and it appears that

their mouths are always
open. Because they are thin

as weeds, the albinos
look hungry. If you drive out

to the farm, tree branches will
point the way. No map will show

where, no phone is listed.
It will seem that the moon, plump

above their shoulders, is constant,
orange as harvest all year

long. We say, when a mother
gives birth to an albino girl,

she feigns sleep after
labor while an Asian

man steals in, spirits
the pale baby away.

Part of the Effect of the Public Scene Is to Importune the Passing Viewer

FOR EXAMPLE:

walking past the Ritz a girl may be sitting on the last step crying
as if alone and you notice, even in this cocktail-hour light, the
little rips and shreds of her chapped lips and that she has no
Kleenex and no one stops to offer one and you feel damned if you
do or don't, not wanting to intrude, as a man is standing maybe
only three feet away, his profile approximating a little shame,
some discomfort, but mostly a sphinx-like composure, or
boredom, perhaps, indicating they *are* together, together in that
way you're not completely sure you'll ever want to know about
again and you're ashamed, too, with nothing to offer but to gaze
intently at the fascinating streetlamp as you walk by.

PROBABLY YOU'VE CAUSED A SCENE YOURSELF:

public or private, at a bar or in a strange apartment, when
suddenly you became conscious of the drama, of the real pleasure
in your tears, the catharsis of the wail and rage, the screams, the
"trashing of the joint," because that's what's next, snipping up
his Liberty of London ties, ripping off her nightgown, pushing
her out naked on the patio for the neighbors' judgment who are
there, to be sure, either by accident or rubbernecked design,
keeping score or scared for their own property. Or instead you've
been the impetus, unfaithful, deceitful, maybe only the hapless
object of some other person's desire thinking that, for all their
protestations of love, you might as well be a bathroom fixture or
bookend. In either case,

[9]

It's Hard to Make a Graceful Exit:

as all scenes peter out in awkward ways. Someone's left thinking
of the perfect remark, a remark that'll sink like an ax blade, the
kind that are never on hand when needed, so that you end up
shouting, spluttering *Oh yeah?! Oh yeah?! Oh Yeah?!* like a moron,
like a damn fool, crying on the last step, in front of strangers,
without a Kleenex.

All Distance

Writing from Boston, where sky is simply
property, a flourish topping crowds
of condos and historic real estate,
I'm trying to imagine blue sky:
the first time, where it happened,
what I was becoming. Being taken there
by car, from a town so newly born that grass
still accounted all distance, an explanation
drawn in measureless yellows, a tone
stubbling the whole world, ten minutes away.

Consider now how the single pussy willow
edging a cattle pond in winter becomes
a wind-shivered monument to what this means,
a placid loneliness asking *nothing, nothing?...*
Not knowing then the proper name for things:
green chubs of milo, the husbandry of soy,
bovine patience, the rhythm of the cud,
sea green foam washing round
a cow's mouth, its tender udders,
the surprise of an animal's dignity...

but something comes before.
Before *car* or *cow*, before
sky becomes...

That sky, I mean, disregarded
as buried memory...

Yes. There was a time before.
Remember when the tiny, sightless hand
could not know, not say *hand*, but knew it

in its straying, knew it in the cool

condensation steaming the station wagon windows,
thrums of heat blowing a brand of idiot's safety
over the brightly-wrapped package
that was then your body, well-loved?

This must have been you, looking out at that world
of flat, buttered fields and blackbirds ascending...

        But what was sky then?

Today, I receive a postcard of
a blue guitar. Here, snow falls with wings,
tumbling in its feathered body, melting
on the window glass. How each evening becomes
another beautiful woman holding
the color of expensive sapphires
against her throat, I'll never know.
It is an ordinary clarity.

        So then was it music?
        Something like love or
        words, a sentimental moment once
        years ago, that blue sky?

How soon the sky and I have grown apart.
On the postcard, an old man hangs
half-dead, strung over his instrument, and what
I have imagined is half-dead, too. Our bones
end hollow, sky blue; the flute comes untuned.

The Spring Burials

Violets growing through the asphalt mean
the usual of spring's predicament:

how, busy getting born, still wings and green
will falter, twist, misgrow their management

and die. Violets grow on one curled leg,
a slender prop obliviously crushed,

and newborn birds are falling from their eggs,
still feathered wet and hidden in the brush

when you walk by. They die in spite of us;
in shoebox nests and jelly jars supplied

with best intentions. Bring them in the house,
then fuss, arrange things, feed them. Occupy

yourself with worms and eyedroppers, sunlight
and potting earth. You'll bury them in days,

feel silly in your grief. And still you'll sit
a moment on the blacktop, study ways

to save an unimportant, pretty weed
or bird. You're still a fool – a fool to bend

so sentimentally and fool in deed,
assuming you know better. Spring is kind.

The Small Sound of
Quiet Animals

The night returns humid, sweating through
the damp curtains, then settles at the baseboards,
beginning the pool of evening.

The single expensive vase, its tulip face now
dark, tilts odd-angled on the desk, asks
for the smallest provocation (it's waited

all day to explode). You give it none.
Your cat is sleeping the shape of answers
into the only comfortable chair,

but let him sleep
because he dreams. His haunches shake.
See the smile of his bared teeth?

*

The man you lived with leaves a note
Scotch-taped to the lampshade. *Gone to Minnesota.*
Please feed my fish. Here's fifteen dollars...

In bed, you smell his boots, leather and sweat
rising from the dark closet doorway.
You think of Blue Earth, Pemberton, Pipestone

and Mankato, his bike a white spot whistling
up the serpentine highway into Minnesota,
the fat, widowed farmers drinking anisette

in municipal bars. You think of their woman

and daughters, straight-backed, Nordic. How they
lie down like angels, Lutheran as the plains.

*

Something bangs in the radiator, heavier
than heat, reminds you how all things
speak, how small sounds come even

from quiet animals. A dresser drawer closes
rooms away. Your Jehovah landlord with a key
to the place? The sisters who fight

over men a floor below? You don't fall
into sleep. No splash, no ripple
to disturb the surface. Kneel into the water,

watch the outline of your leg disappear,
then finger, forearm and elbow. Curl yourself
fetal on the empty bed. The shape of a fist.

Outside the Hotel Ritz

The ripped girl gathers herself,
draws into the recess of a downtown
highrise, then cries as if alone into
the body of an indifferent building.

The black feathers of her party dress
forsake her, dead flutter falling round
her arms. Having flown through many autumns,
in other clear, martini dusks, their circles

kept growing smaller till they settled
at nothing, save decoration. Now currents
are senseless and wind, still sweeping warm
across the public ponds, just wind.

Around the corner a man in a tuxedo looks
bored, always waiting. She's borrowed
his handkerchief. Profile of the Napoleonic
sphinx, yes. Yet something struggles

beneath the dial of his face. He craves
the crowd, its wandering breach and flow,
hears a genuine laugh bob up and wants
to follow it home, all the way through

the city, to any lit place beyond him. Night
is pending. Its tributaries flow, spilling
fast onto the sidewalk; something wet and plumed
to catch him. Like feathers raining. Like wings.

Names You Can't Pronounce

I

Another summer in a town you know
like the backs of your knees and just
as sweaty. Nights aren't much cooler.

Sometimes, when you walk out late to think
or just stare at your hands swinging
next to you, the green smells

of the Russian olive surrounding
the synagogue push at the back
of your throat. Too big a mouthful,

so you stare at your hands which are
swinging soft and pale at the end
of your wrists and listen to cicadas
chorus their unknown tragedy.

II

You have two lovers. One knows you best
but his hands are soft, pale, female
like your own. The other tastes the back

of your knees, but won't make love
to you. You stare at his knuckles
when he works, square and browned

from summer jobs. With the first
you take long walks past the synagogue
to a park with a war memorial.

[17]

The names there are thin, tragedy
chipped into black marble: Cassavettes,
Beacom, a Russian name you can't pronounce,
all of these men, to you, unknown.

III

You can see the synagogue from
the window of your bedroom, wake
to the sign: FREEDOM FOR SOVIET JEWS.

The women downstairs have made love
and now they fight. It's a tragedy,
they were friends before

they were lovers. The man living in
the basement is old, a veteran. Says
he hates Krauts, likes Russians.

The summer mornings are soft and pale
and when you wake from sleep
your hands flutter against the sheet;
the backs of your knees ache.

Rondeau at the Train Stop

It bothers me: the genital smell of the bay
drifting toward me on the T stop, the train
circling the city like a dingy, year-round
Christmas display. The Puritans were right! Sin
is everywhere in Massachusetts, hell-bound

in the population. It bothers me
because it's summer now and sticky – no rain
to cool things down; heat like a wound
that will not close. Too hot, these shameful
percolations of the body that bloom
between strangers on a train. It bothers me

now that I'm alone and singles foam
around the city, bothered by the lather, the rings
of sweat. Know this bay's a watery animal, hind-end
perpetually raised: a wanting posture, pain
so apparent, wanting so much that it bothers me.

The Hideous Chair

This hideous,
upholstered in gift-wrap fabric, chromed
in places, design possibility

for the future canned ham.
Its genius
wonderful, circa 1993.

I've assumed a great many things:
the perversity of choices, affairs
I did or did not have.

But let the record show
that I was happy.
O let the hideous chair

stand! For the Chinese apothecary
with his roots and fluids;
for Raoul at the bank;

for the young woman in Bailey's Drug,
expert on henna; and Warren Beatty,
tough, sleek stray. For Fluff and Flo,

drunk at noon, and the Am Vets lady
reading her *Vogue*, the cholos
on the corner where the 57 bus comes by,

for their gratifying, cool appraisal
and courtly manner when I pass.
Let the seat be comfortable

but let the chair be hideous
and stand against the correct,
hygienic, completely proper

subdued in taxidermied elegance.
Let me have in any future
some hideous thing to love,

here Boston, MA, 8 Farrington Ave.

II

For Catherine:
Juana, Infanta of Navarre

Ferdinand was systematic when
he drove his daughter mad.

With a Casanova's careful art,
he moved slowly,
stole only one child at a time
through tunnels specially dug
behind the walls of her royal
chamber, then paid the Duenna
well to remember nothing
but his appreciation.

Imagine how quietly
the servants must have worked,

loosening the dirt, the muffled
ring of pick-ends against
the castle stone. The Duenna,
one eye gauging the drugged girl's
sleep, each night handing over
another light parcel, another
small body vanished
through the mouth of a hole.

Once you were a daughter, too,
then a wife and now the mother
of a baby with a Spanish name.

Paloma, you call her, *little dove;*
she sleeps in a room beyond you.

[25]

Your husband, too, works late,
drinks too much at night, comes
home lit, wanting sex and dinner.
You feign sleep, shrunk
in the corner of the queen-sized bed.

You've confessed, you can't feel things
when they touch you;

take Prozac for depression, Ativan
for the buzz. Drunk, you call your father
who doesn't want to claim
a half sand-nigger grandkid.
He says he never loved your mother.

No one remembers Juana; almost
everything's forgotten in time,

and if I tell her story,
it's only when guessing
what she loved, what she dreamed
about, the lost details of a life
that barely survives history.

God and Latin, I suppose, what she loved.
And dreams of mice pouring out
from a hole. The Duenna, in spite
of her black, widow's veil, leaning
to kiss her, saying *Juana, don't listen...*

Another Poem for Mothers

Mother, I'm trying
to write
a poem to you –

which is how most
poems to mothers must
begin – or, *What I've wanted*

to say, Mother... but we
as children of mothers,
even when mothers ourselves,

cannot bear our poems
to them. Poems to
mothers make us feel

little again. How to describe
that world that mothers spin
and consume and trap

and love us in, that spreads
for years and men and miles?
Those particular hands that could

smooth anything: butter on bread,
cool sheets or weather. It's
the wonder of them, good or bad,

those mother-hands that pet
and shape and slap,
that sew you together

the pieces of a better house
or life in which you'll try
to live. Mother,

I've done no better
than the others, but for now,
here is your clever failure.

Bee Sting

With bees, it isn't the sting itself
but the unprovoked attack
that lingers.

How unfair to walk unwary, barefoot
on hot concrete, simply
pleasuring your feet,
or stepping down on a beach towel

only to be assaulted by the small plot
of something you meant no harm to.
That first pain is learned the hard way:

at five, you call
all-y, all-y, all come free
singing blind into a hive
hidden in the swing-set's pole, then fall

what seemed the longest
fall; a cloud of bees flowered from your lips.

And later, put to bed with ice
and ointments melting over
the welts that covered you,

there was no explaining the bees'
behavior, no way to comprehend the reason
in their rage. You may never understand

this: the will behind the stinger,
a certain, fatal anger to survive.

FROM *The Exploding Madonna*

— *She was incomprehensible, for, in her, soul and spirit were one — the beauty of her body was the essence of her soul. She was that unity sought for by philosophers through many centuries. In this outdoor waiting room of winds and stars she had been sitting for a hundred years at peace in the contemplation of herself. It became known to her, at length, that she was to be born again. Sighing, she began a long conversation with a voice that was in the white wind, a conversation which took many hours and of which I can give only a fragment here...*

BEAUTY: (*Her lips scarcely stirring, her eyes turned, as always, inward upon herself*)

Whither shall I journey now?...

I. THE ADDRESS

Beauty, your copper-colored face floats up
Then down, mirrors from the base of the candle,
Mimics my face, my eyes, my hair and hands;
Fetal little pig-me buoyed in the crystal,
Amniotic waters reflecting
From the mantle. But I'm no Beauty, I've let
That go, allowed the shock to fracture through
A pulled plug more live than we've ever been.
I'm named rightly for the dog-faced Furies,
Avengers of Demeter's mythic mood;
My father never grasps the happy
Accident of his choice. Cliché, you say?

Another dirty father? Look around,
Beauty, Demeter's rage still floods the headlines
Every day, cause célèbre of *People*
Magazine; little girls grown fat and sad
Or sadly glamorous remembering,
Forgetting, where their fathers' hands have lain.
Think of it, Beauty – a voice like a ball
Forever bouncing: shadow in the hall,
Shadow on the stairs, shadow that you'll take
To bed. So in a moment, Beauty, I will stand
Up, taking hold of the candlestick, and
Tapping gently, separating white from yolk,
Release you in my palm. This will be a trick,
– a most difficult illusion, to leave
The body, here, in my chair, nodding – to slip
Away quiet, quiet as a dimmed light, holding
You still, nervous mercury, dividing
And dividing in the quarters of my
Hot hand. Don't be afraid, I like your face,
No matter what some mirrors tell us, and,
If you concentrate, the voice grows dimmer,
Dissolving to the smallest parts of speech:
Tagmeme, phoneme, the skeleton bare and
Bleached, picked serene from corrupted sound,
Syllables filling with hot molecules,
Agitated word-balloons popping into
Language that came before all prefixes,
Before the final loss of pure quiet.
I'll take you anywhere you want to go,
I'll catch you up on everything you've missed,
Beauty. Be ready when I give the signal.
We'll go silent. *No one will ever know.*

II. An Annunciation

*...the ascension of his wife's body above the target
area, Exploding Madonna of the weapons range,
was a celebration of the rectilinear intervals through
which he perceived the surrounding continuum of time
and space. Here she became one with the madonnas of
the hoardings and the ophthalmic films, the Venus of
the magazine cuttings whose postures celebrated his
own search through the suburbs of hell...*

I have snapshots in my wallet wrapped in
A plastic case, next to credit cards:
Visa, MasterCard, American Express;
Millions of dots matrixed into Mother, Father,
Brother, Daughter, their faces swaddled
In dollar bills. When you look at this one
Think Ingrid Bergman, circa *Notorious,*
Dewy drunk, with Devlin's handkerchief tied
About her waist, before the karate
Chop but without the rose filter. Add
A more pragmatic nose, a more generous
Profile, an extra inch of curving bosom
Like soft, grainless bread in my father's hands.
In this photo he's from the movies, too,
As everything eventually is.
Night of the Iguana cabana boy,
A touchingly sinister pompadour
Sculpted above his forehead. They're dancing.
They're pressed close to each other, one breath
Between them, thigh exploring thigh. They will
Make love and she will be a virgin;
The Testimony: look closely – delicate
Brush strokes drawn with blood in the pure lines
Of a Japanese character; dark ink
Indelibly defining a white sheet.

I'm not yet born somewhere. I sit shelved:
Narrating soul, crap-shooter of dual fates,
Untimely gag gift chosen from a file,
Love Child of the Supremes' Top Forty hit;
(there's war in Rhodesia, riots ending in Watts),
Bastard of the Birchwood Country Club
Fox trot, backseat tango in the parking lot.
At five, I was as spoiled as the new decade:
Daringly pre-dysfunctional daughter
Of the 1970s, split-level,
Incest-and-Manhattans patio crowd.
It's Love American Style, so I
Took this photograph myself. You can see
My shadow, my thumb obscuring the window
Of the lens, my childish silhouette
A murder-scene outline against the wall.
But here, tonight, they're dancing, as lanterns
Drench the floor; his hands fleetingly at peace
In the folds of her yellow gown. They love
Each other. Tonight, they love each other.
Look at the picture. My mother. Father...

III: THE HOUR OF LEAD

...First – Chill – then Stupor – then the letting go – ...

The chrome shines until it stings, reflecting
The women's sad asses as they shuffle
In papery gowns from the locker room:
Fun house butts or the elongated and
Elegantly dead derrières of a
Mannerist's pietà, depending on
How kind the angle, how soft the focus.
The big blonde nurse is a sugar mountain
Inserting IVs all around the room.
Hair spun to confection, sticky in sea-foams,

[33]

Girded in an arsenal of pastels,
She reviews the proper method for mounting
The gurneys – *Place both hands on the side guards,*
Then lift and scooch, swinging the legs over
Onto the bed. She demonstrates scooching.
The blue paper gowns chatter uniformly,
Obediently. Each woman reviews
The advice she's been given by her friends.

1. *Ignore the first sound you'll hear. It's just*
   Machines separating blood from plasma.
2. *There are two doctors. Ask for LaBenz. The one*
   Who looks like Trapper John on TV.
3. *Head for the escorts in the orange vests.*
   Keep your head down and just keep walking. They can't
   Come across the sidewalk. Wear sunglasses,
   Maybe a hat, and don't look at the signs.
4. *Make sure you bring cash. No checks accepted.*
5. *Pay the extra for the anesthesia.*

One woman is thinking of an old Greek
Philosopher, how his students must have
Hated him, stolen his ideas, maybe
Even went to bed with him only for
The grade, and how this ancient philosopher
Must have known they mocked him, those beautiful
Young men, so smooth, and how it filled him with
Shame but, still, he couldn't stop, the ways he loved
Them, adored their soft hands and conversation,
Their white tunics brushing at the knees.
Another woman, a very young woman, is
Thinking of the boyfriend she's left sitting
Somewhere, out there, somewhere past the surgical,
Sitting in a chair, his hands together,
Fingers steepled over his crotch. She is
Thinking about the night they slept naked

Under the big screen TV, thinking of
The way the colors blurred over their skin;
Pale green, then red, yellow, all the colors,
Bleeding and separating, then coming
Together, one hue bruised onto their bodies.
Next to her a woman is fascinated
By the needle pushed into the vein
Snaking across the top of her wrist,
The small pucker of skin around its entry
Point, the cold sensation of the drip
Burning up her arm. She consoles herself
By making a hierarchy of pain: *less than*
Having your ears pierced, less than having your
Teeth cleaned, less than getting a tattoo...
Top Forty hits float down from speakers hidden
In the ceiling: Whitney Houston wants to know
If he *really* loves her; Mötley Crüe reveals
She goes down good. When the doctor comes through
The double doors at the far end of the room,
He speaks softly to the women, holds someone's
Hand as the gurneys wheel past, then disappear.

(*Epigraph and inserted text fragments taken from F. Scott Fitzgerald,*
J.G. Ballard, Don DeLillo and Emily Dickinson)

[35]

Erections

When first described imperfectly
by my shy mother, I tried to leap

from the moving
car. A response,

I suspect, of not
just terror (although

a kind of terror continues to play
its part), but also a mimetic gesture,

the expression equal
to a body's system of absurd

jokes and dirty stories.
With cockeyed breasts

peculiar as distant cousins,
and already the butt of the body's

frat-boy humor,
I'd begun to pack

a bag, would set off
soon for my separate

country. Now, sometimes,
I admire the surprised engineering:

how a man's body can rise,
squaring off with the weight

of gravity, single-minded,
exposed as the blind

in traffic. It's the body leaping
that I praise, vulnerable

in empty space.
It's mapping the empty

space; a man's life driving
down a foreign road.

Rose Red

She never wanted the troll,

though, when freeing his beard
trapped in the bill of a circling bird,
when sliding her scissors through the soft
hairs at the nub of his chin, she did
think the shadow dropping from the gull's
wings lent his face a certain ugly interest.

She never wanted the prince's brother,

second prize to the elder, but just as vain,
with a woman's soft hips and hands,
surrounding himself with mirrors and liking
her sister better anyway, her indiscriminate
sweetness: an ordinary fruit ripening
in a bowl displayed on a public table.

And she did not want the bear

their mother invited next to the fire,
though his stinking fur could make
her eyes and mouth water. Once, she devised
a way to lie beside him, innocently
at first, then not so, curled behind him,
running her thumbnail down his spine.

What she wanted, of course, was her own place in the forest,

where she would take the flowering trees
that grew outside her mother's bedroom window –
one white, buxom with albino blossoms,

[38]

one red, smaller, with delicate, hooked thorns –
and plant them on opposite sides of her cottage,
watching each bloom fall as summer spoiled them.

Ordinary Storm

I've built this for you   It stands
as a shore against Time which is
after all   like water

           just as seamless in motion
           as it is in repose

constant

soaking equally
everything through

so that each rushing moment is busy
indiscriminate   sinking

           the moment before

I've built this to confirm   what becomes
insignificant: our lives

(which really are not
mutual   already loosened
and untying the ravel of slip-
knots they've made together)

the room   and its window
from which we watched
one ordinary

storm

No matter   it will remain
that cloud banks

           deepened to the bruise

[40]

of hydrangea

threads of lightning strung
the sleeping neighborhood

a sky-sized web
and that your hand   (fluttering pulse
                    heart of the hummingbird)
found
the hollow

        above my hip   and rested.

The Green That Never Leaves the Skin

Omne animal post coitum triste

Any neighbor can hear
the broken sound that slides
through the windows, eyes
regular and white as the moon,

that sound like dark grass
rising in the face of lovers
who've passed through on the way
to their own great need.

For some, it's the way a child
has no sense of what's clean.
He sees her pick the sand
between her toes, then rub the grain

away, return it to the air
like a gift he'd given her.
His secret is in the sound
that comes from basement windows

late at night. His love burns
through his gut, above him wakes
dark water in neighbors
with their own burns singing.

For another, the woman next
door who's begun to add seasons
like a cribbage score, the sound
is carried in the lawn boys

down on bended knees all spring,
the milk of dandelions drying
to their work gloves. The green
never leaves their skin.

The woman next door closes
her drapes, fades into the grey
tasks of her day. Her ears close
to the green wave that slides

through her windows. Long nights
she will listen to her neighbors,
their daughters, who begin to hum
the excellent sound of sleep.

Prayer for Men

I will not praise your body after sex
naked on the small, white bed

as prayer is sent to gods, and you,
thin-boned and sleeping,

vulnerable to my hands and mouth,
are too humane for ancient games.

If you had come a whirl of smoke, deified
exhausted fire, turned inside me

burning till my tongue learned flames,
then I might praise you.

If you had put on feathers and descended,
pulled me into sky or water, hung me

weightless, pinned inside your beating wing,
then I might praise you.

But you entered the way a man is made to
enter, asked my name, then waited

for an answer the way men do. It's praise
to watch you listen in your sleep, to fit

the curve your body questions; praise enough
to guard you until morning. Then gods will

lie down on mountaintops and dream their human
dreams of prayer, of women, of love.

[44]

The Problem of Fidelity

It's the gamble, of course –
the way a shot slips down when sent
by a stranger; the conversation

which, in itself, says nothing
but all that isn't said; watching
how a man takes off his shirt,

unbuttons either collar
or cuffs first or pulls the whole
affair over, not careful about

anything. How exciting was it?
Hiding in the closet, that humiliated
voice, raging, at the door;

the other man, stunned and lying
for you? Even now memory
makes you shake, reminds you

how you almost lost, how
one small breath, the tingle
of a hanger, might have changed

three lives for worse
or better. Never knowing.
That's the way games work:

one outcome, one life. A bet
concludes, another's placed
as someone flips a card. Face up.

A Sleeping Man Must
Be Awakened to Be Killed

All afternoon I thought the decision must fall
between two abstractions:

what is merciful
versus
what is honorable;

whether to wake the sleeping man before
they kill him, or not. I confess

my interest wasn't
noble. The morning news
unfolded in details which,

unfortunately, fascinate: a tiny camera hidden
in a teapot he'd requested,

by which they saw him count
his many sticks of dynamite,
booby-trap the entryways

then fall into an agitated sleep; the dilemma
of children as hostages. What got to me, finally,

was how young the kids were,
only three and four. I pictured
them in a yellow schoolroom,

looking lost, helplessly cranky,
a piano on wheels in one corner.

This day passes. We make dinner,
love; you escape into your own dreams.
It occurs to me, now studying your shut

eyed flutters, your left hand gripping and releasing
the humid sheet, that what is planned

is practical, must be, directed
by those with practical concerns.
I wonder what they are? I wonder

who decides to wake the sleeping man, maybe dreaming,
maybe lost in the white space between dreams.

What reason to shake him back to where he's gotten
now: this yellow schoolroom, a piano on
wheels? I watch you sleep. You don't answer.

Love Poem

There are too many similes for bed –
nothing at all like the things I've said
scribbling late this last hour;

not like the boats I've rigged, or rivers either,
designed for us to float. Metaphor
sinks what I meant to say.

And about what Rilke says, I know even
his angels won't save me now; heaven
is much too terrible to leave.

So all you get to know is that I'm trying,
my tongue not a stupid girl crying
down my throat, wet and speechless.

[48]

The Sadness of Infidels

That which illuminates is sometimes only sad;
this full moon's rule, titular

at best, and each decision
we come to beneath her, obscured,

vague as the myth inside a constellation.

We're more comfortable with vanishing,
the partial beliefs of a bedside lamp,

and only trust in what we must
keep hidden. We make love our euphemism.

I've observed each part of me eclipse
as your body passes over mine,

your mouth moving then replacing nipple and clit,

desire circling a single point, unanchored,
incapable of resting or sinking in.

We're sad as glaciers are, who cannot feel this,

propelled by the engine of their frozen weight,
natural machines made completely of mirrors,

we put out the light, moving forward and blind.

The Real Animal

...but next to you
again sitting
near you (very)
in the dark again
I consider how
next to you I envy
the real animals   how

next to you
even the mangiest bitch
who dons her passion
loud as the pattern
in a houndstooth coat
could get next to you

sniff you   howl
and breathe and shove
herself right up
to you push
into you
unwrap you with the wet
nap of her raw silk
nose   But next to you

in its studied
pose your right hand knows
though civilized
though knuckled hard
though bent
with speaking fingers
I'm next to you
won't speak though native

[50]

tongued   articulate
might say has said before
I'll touch you
here   next here
but still unquiet
as a bird perched
next to me
unsettled near me

in the dark   again
it's Now
before the moments gone
I want to make you
hear it say it
very clear
I'm next to you
I'm next to you
I'm next to you...

You Come Too...

Franconia, N.H., 1993

With no geography to name these wild,
phallic flowers,
or Latin phrase for the skeptical
blackbird arranging
his deep coat against the wind,

it's a moment before you're willing
to believe what I tell you,
A *love poem*...
Soon, we'll agree,
what is simple may last:

a blackbird ordering his feathers
in the polish of evening sun,
these wild, phallic flowers
scattering the mountain,
a hand resting lightly

on your thigh
as we turn to drive away.

Tick

Remind me of a similar devotion;

how the head, buried
deeply in the brush

and gully of damp flesh,
becomes platonic
in its gratefulness,

a perfect worship.
This is why one body,
fastened to the forest

of another, swells.
This wild dependence

of the host on her guest.

III

The Man Who Tried to Rape You

When he appears a block away, you know.
Like when you watch a made-for-TV movie
and guess the ending in a minute,

or how, if you're listening, you'll almost hear
a pulse, a muted beat inside your head,
announcing the return of what's been coming.

Surprisingly, you think, it takes the form
of what's most obvious: the backlit shape
of trouble – first a faceless outline,

as if whoever drew this couldn't find
the way to fill it in, the buzzing mist
of streetlamps making ghosts of all his edges.

And then that ghost you've always feared is coming,
is walking toward you up the sidewalk, up
from childhood and books and all the movies

with which you've ever scared yourself, purposeless
as ghosts are, vaguely sad and understanding
in a way, as if he, too, knows a thing

about what's inevitable. The pause
before he grabs for you is awkward as
a school dance. It's like that, you think, a dance:

his arms heavy at your waist, the way he
smells not unpleasant, pulls you toward
his hips, which, in another case, might please

or thrill you. But now that thrill is fear, or
maybe it always was. The dance goes on
a moment more and you're not screaming, only

saying No and No and No; this becomes
a rhythm, like breathing, just as quiet,
as if you'll go on saying No forever,

and then he stops. Lets go. You wonder later
if it's your business to be generous.
And that you're sad and frightened, but not angry.

And where he went, pathetic silhouette,
the man who walked away, back to the dark;
how, after, even streetlamps seemed too bright

to fall on him. His face turning away.

The Dream, After Surgery

for Carl Phillips

You can say fever and codeine
make these dreams more tangible,

that this is not the life
for Russian mystics or portent:
the human-headed lion,
the owl who speaks in tongues...

but it takes a pattern anyway,
in the shape of flavors pooled
at the back of a mouth in which
the hollow sockets still mourn

the best-removed but
tender part of themselves.
Isn't it always like this when,
suddenly, something is cut away?

A dream in which each organ, shell,
or aborted attempt tries to right itself,
and, when unable, floats helplessly
separate in a cold jar? No

matter if we try to gather
everything that's taken from us,
named officially by Linnaeus
or any other famous collector,

still pieces are lost.

The dream is a dream of returning,
of figuring to make it whole.

Georgic on Sitting Still

for Kay Auxier-Horwath

Kay sits still in front of student artists
twice a week. She is thin, they complain,
she casts no shadows, no purple crease below
her buttocks, or valley disappearing
to become her breasts. She says, *It's hard
to sit still, it takes an athlete. To them I'm just
an odalisque, reclining.* I say, *try this:*

lie naked on the bed. Place one arm
flat against the coolness
of the covers, let the other settle
into the hollow above your hip. Listen.

Here is how the body forgets
itself. The pulse starts, flutters
a panicked beat inside your thigh. When
your stomach begins to moan
like something locked alone in a room
without windows, go past this.

Go past your sweating palms,
the tremor of your muscles.
Imagine pennies on your eyelids,
Brando's dead wife in *Last Tango*
surrounded by flowers.

Copy the stillness of eggs, the ecstasy
of monks, the morbid sleep
of content children. Imagine you float

in a jar on a shelf in the great
Sisters of Mercy hospital. Look.
Now you are sitting still.

Teaching Madeleine to Swim

Like the everlasting schools
of Darter, Musk, and Angel,
you're in water

but there's no god
with trident, no rescue of the lost,
no mouth-to-mouth for the drowned.

You want to float,
desperate with the first wave,
dissolve, like a shell

held by water
as by lovers. Let it
take you down, Madeleine,

let go, it
always wins. This
weight contains the ghost I

cradle in my arms; you
and the place to put your faith in.

Lullaby for a Russian Painter

Elena, lay your head
down. Let the floating

face, unfinished, rest
upon the wall. Tend

the painted girl who chafes
inside your frame

with another canvas.
Stretch it blank enough

to offer her a small, oiled
picture of somewhere better,

a release from that O
puzzling her painted mouth...

sleep, Elena. You're tired now
from picking up those

bodies, drawn but never
settled. Put them down.

In your dreams no telephone
will ring, letters go unopened,

all the sad citizens of Moscow
sit down for good black tea.

The Rescue Ship

In memoriam, for J.G.

My dead friend Joe is dressed
for travel, and, having been
particular in life, would think
this will not quite do.

In this last station,
a suburban mortuary,
ceremony is ranch-styled
and everything is wrong:

the bad, blue suit and
politicians' hair molded
into place by the morgue
cosmetologist; dusty mums,
their bovine faces mooning
like soft-headed cousins
at a family reunion.
The stitches visible
between the lips,
concealed at the wrists.

His family builds a pyramid
of grief walking from the open casket,
they stutter, pause, then start again,
stammer their confused procession.
A Siamese dance in its connected
sorrow, they recall that gesture
on Géricault's raft, the survivors sailed
here now, still locked to impossible lives,

the blue flocked paper on the mortuary
walls wedding sea and sky forever.

But here, no rescue ship is coming,
not scheduled for arrival;
no hand to signal the heroes,
or dot on the horizon speeding forward
with hot tea, blankets, bandages or balm. No.
What they have is flowers at their feet –

as they stumble past the pews,
past the kneeling people
whose lips and cheeks shine hot,
reflect the colors of the stained
glass saints hovering overhead,
distant and immune in their mild
robes and opaque, pastel halos –

only flowers and more flowers, the lowing
of the mums, their grins already drooping,
dying in the August sauna. They surrender
each final scent as their perfumes rise toward
heaven from a static garden below the paper sky.

How the Elderly Drive

You'd think this piece of road
just a dream for the old
woman coaxing her Bonneville
like a dangerous ghost down I-80.

Only her head appears above
the door panel, disembodied
by sundown, floating somewhere
above the thin string of her neck.

The way the elderly drive,
with their disheartened climbs
and slow-motioned maneuvers, it seems
they've only a mile to go down

soft, dirt roads, so that even Aunt
Pearl, her head sawed neatly from
her shoulders on the interstate last
winter, smiled down at the salad

she brought home from the luncheon
instead of tapping her brakes
gently when the semi tried to merge.
You'd think old people had no sense

of speed or the lateness of the day, or
where we all must get to, their magnified
eyes peering, inscrutable above
their steering wheels, tuberous hands

shaking, faintly shaking,
guiding their phantoms home.

[67]

On Being Disregarded
by the Famous

Once, in Omaha, you let it go

over Tanqueray at an outdoor pub,
that sometimes, on the subway in New York,

you carry a handgun, wondering how

your secret changes you from the others
riding, both malignant and benign, to

the outer boroughs. Because you're

certified with agent, friends in the same
predicament, who also like to hunt,

write and marry tough, attractive women

who take their grief but always hand it back,
I've found knowing you a little grand,

a thought to fondle on the spiritless night

of Sunday mornings, when life's wrong
or simply dull. A guilty, silly pleasure

then, as if it rectifies the place we're from,

the shabby education or total
lack of grace; hard to admit, but mostly

not destructive. Remember, *It's a good*

life if you don't give in, or so our
mutual acquaintance always said.

The Silver Tree

Will you believe that the silver tree
has emptied its seed inside you?

Why, then, do we wake to the calculus
of strange roots beneath our sheet?

They brought us to where it grew, foolish and costly, dear to the
two men who had purchased it, made it their silver elm child,
fantasy of a small boy, monument to what is worst, most hidden
and, therefore, loved in each parent. The simple tree that Fabergé
might dream for Anastasia, but never fashion because of this
simplicity, or dream George Emerson must have of climbing –
to bellow everlastingly, to tumble from his perch into the narcotic
bed of an Italian poppy field: raw glow of metal branch, flame of
the foiled leaves, where it stood, a jewel set in the tiara of the
Maine coast, and beneath, how the ocean dimly glittered in
comparison, tossed like a woman's envy...

Is this the disease of a beautiful life?

Or, conversely, is this beautiful life the disease?

...and we drank red wine inside their love-house, made complete
with mirrors on every surface, doubling, refracting, alert to the
possibility that happiness might be captured, and everywhere in
the rooms we heard its transparent wing beating at the windows.
Later we walked the property, admiring the garden, then down
to the water where the sun dropped its boiling fist just below the
horizon and floated under like something peacefully drowned.
It was hard for us to return to the city, where the sky is dissected

[70]

and the admonition of a grocery cart groans constantly from the
street. Hard to speak of this, *wanting*, the grand variety of wishes
that seem needs here.

You iron the perfection of a stiff,
white shirt for tomorrow, and I carry

    my cigarettes to the window, blow
    secret smoke out into the neighborhood.

The Death of Humphrey Bogart

This moment, I can't recall exactly which,
but there's a sect of Buddhists who believe one's
version of heaven lasts only as long as his
name is remembered on earth. Then, if this watch
truly times what's billed as eternal, add heaven
to that list of life's disappointments – all hype,
no finish. Women know the aphorism:
it's easy to fall for an ugly man. Your type,
Bogie, with your sad, gargoyle profile
and fidgety pistol, the hair-trigger style
of you sipping your gin with killers and dolls,
lips curled back from the glass. Who'd call that a smile?

     *   *   *

Baby? Where are you?

It's after Christmas time, 1956,
       when a young woman, eyes
like a leopard's cub, lies quiet on the other side
of the bed.
       Nearly all this night she's watched
her husband pick at his chest, the laboring itch
of the very sick.

She doesn't know it yet, but already she's settled
       on Psalm 23, white roses,
the fresh, green leaves of their own magnolia,
to salt the ocean with ashes.

This morning the wind tangles
       a thin whistle in

the trees outside their bedroom window. Soon

other women will rise, with newspapers and husbands
on their way to business...

*

...During the service, her mind may drift, wondering
if heaven has a kidney-shaped pool,

a barbecue, burgers grilled pink in the middle, a painted
sunset eternally bobbing on
a sound stage of perfect, pacific horizon:

Prayers are being read:

>...He will receive blessing
>from the Lord and vindication
>from the God of his salvation.
>Such is the generation of those
>who seek Him...

She can picture them together at poolside
the Nivens coming for cocktails at five
Frank soon to arrive with the broad he's brought

round; platinum haired, stacked like an angel,
an attitude of kisses, well-placed
and meaningfully red, forever at her lips.

ERIN BELIEU was born in 1965 in Omaha, Nebraska, and educated at the University of Nebraska, Ohio State University, and Boston University. In addition to winning the National Poetry Series, she has received the Academy of American Poets Prize. She is managing editor at AGNI and lives in Cambridge, Massachusetts.

Book design and composition by John D. Berry, using Aldus PageMaker 5.0 and a Macintosh IIVX. The type is Quadraat, an original digital typeface designed by Fred Smeijers and released in 1992 by FontShop International as part of their FontFont type library. Quadraat displays the subtle irregularities of a handmade face, which make it particularly readable at small sizes and give it a distinctive character at large sizes.

The new Copper Canyon Press logo is the Chinese character for poetry, and is pronounced shi. It is composed of two simple characters: the righthand character is the phonetic and means "temple" or "hall," while the lefthand character means "speech" or "word." The calligraphy is by Yim Tse, who teaches at the University of British Columbia.